mystic turf

poems

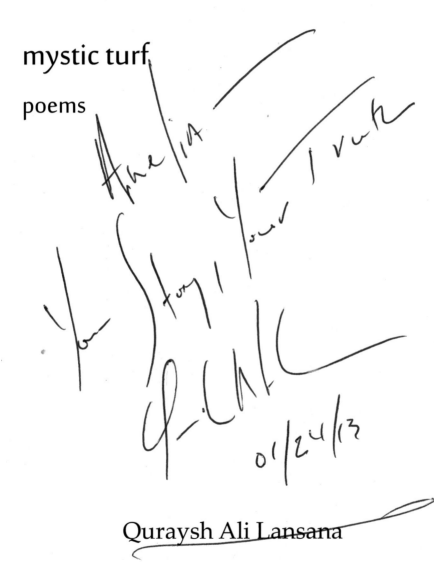

Quraysh Ali Lansana

mystic turf

Editor: Randall Horton
Cover art: "Breathless" by Felicia Grant Preston, mixed medium
Author photo: Glodean Champion Photography

ISBN 978-0-9852877-5-7

LCCN 2012949389

Willow Books, a Division of Aquarius Press
PO Box 23096
Detroit, MI 48223
www.WillowLit.com

Printed in the United States of America

Contents

scent
touch
sight
sound
taste

III.   where we live

IV.   parting water

Grateful acknowledgement is made to the editors of the following publications, in which versions of these poems originally appeared:

The New Sound: A Journal of Interdisciplinary Art & Literature, Spring 2011: "blind" and "this is not a political poem (it's about vermin)"
Tuesday; An Art Project, Ninth Issue, Spring 2011: "safe"
ELEVEN ELEVEN, Issue 11, Fall 2011: "african america"
Sou'wester, Spring 2010: "dead dead"
After Hours: A Journal of Chicago Writing and Art, 10th Anniversary Issue, Summer 2010: "september eleven, two-thousand and two"
TriQuarterly Online, Summer 2010: "lonely offices"
Another Chicago Magazine, Summer 2010: "mama sense: an elegy"
The American Poetry Review, May/June 2009: "blur" and "playing hooky"
bloodsoil (sooner red) (Voices from the American Land, Vol.1, No. 2, Spring 2009): "government springs," "face: harvest," "face: after harvest," "anadarko blue," "haunted" and "crescent, ok"
Exact Change Only, Volume 1, Issue 1, April 2009: "gully"
Reverie: Midwest African American Literature, Fall 2008/Vol.2: "eighth grade," "reverse commute," and "wedlock"
A Writers' Congress: Chicago Poets on Barack Obama's Inauguration (The DePaul Poetry Institute, 2009): "sport"
The Drunken Boat, Cave Canem Issue 2008, Vol. 8, Issues III-IV: "body shop"
Tuesday; An Art Project, Fourth Issue, Fall 2008: "pilgrimage"
Make: A Chicago Literary Magazine, Summer/Fall 2007: "mascot"
Another Chicago Magazine, Summer 2007: "On the Day of the Harmonic Convergence"
Cave Canem 10 X 10 (Summer 2006): "catdaddy"
AnthologY-Visiting Authors, Winter-Spring 2005 (Downtown Writer's Voice of the Syracuse YMCA, 2005): "nature"
Ink and Ashes, Fall 2005: "halloween"
Cave Canem Anthology VIII/2003: "crack house"
The Comstock Review, Vol. 16, #2, Fall/Winter 2002: "running in place"
Role Call: A Generational Anthology of Social and Political Black Literature & Art (Third World Press, 2002): "smolder" and "public school"
Obsidian III, Vol. 2, #1 (North Carolina State University Press, 2000): "cleaning graves in calvert"
360-A Revolution of Black Poets (Blackwords/Runagate Press, 1998): "crutch" and "give and go"

Thanks to Randall Horton, Diane Seuss, Adrian Matejka, Major Jackson, Georgia A. Popoff, Renny Golden, Patricia Smith, Phil Memmer, Cheri Taylor, Gregory Pardlo, Patricia Spears Jones, Matthew Shenoda, Samantha Thornhill and Cave Canem for insight in shaping these poems and kicking me in the arse when necessary.

this dedication page is ancestral burial ground
this dedication page is looking over your shoulder

as for the living, this book is for my siblings:

Wanda "Bonnie" Myles-Lynch
Dr. Charolette Myles-Nixon
William "Champ" Myles
Sharon Renee "Cookie" Myles
Diane "Dede" Henderson-White

I.   earthen pulpit

mascot

for zack. for mark.

I.

the red undertones that inform my melanin
were birthed in the black mountain foothills
near the tennessee-mississippi border.

my great grandfather albert found freedom
just before the trail of tears migration
and hooked up with an ornery black
woman in westpoint, muddy waters' neighbor.

ms. cora mae, never one to hold anything
long but money, sent him to his horse
upon the news—she had things to do—my grandma
would join the family business in a while.

ms. cora mae carried three daughters and two sons
into post-reconstruction mississippi, sown
from different seeds. the women, their doors
always open, were sexy to kill for. the men
loyal enough to do the job—cooking shine and running
game.
            when the klan came calling the guns were loaded.
my father and uncles, all under ms. cora mae's command
led rebellion against attack on their cottage industry, left
red cotton to feed brittle soil, then scattered in four directions.

after three draft dodging years in miami, daddy ended
up in oklahoma, where his sisters somehow landed
and his mama joined them after california.

II.

i am an okie. grew up on cherokee
as did zack, my first best friend,
who lived two blocks away and wore
the street in his skin. we liked basketball,
cars, and never watched westerns.
zack disappeared in high school after one year
in warpaint riding a spotted mare at pre-game.
he was gone before i had the chance
to tell him what i already knew.

grandma never claimed native and hated
anyone darker than a grocery bag. this is where
i begin, on cherokee, trying to find zack
to talk about this mascot issue.

III.

the beantown honkies
the johnson city jarheads
the washington senators
the oaktown wannabees
the cushing crackers
the tulsa rednecks
the old baltimore bigots
the chicago police department
the white city afrikaaners
the cook county overseers
the heritage foundation
the riverside peckerwoods
the german shepherds

IV.

How politically correct can we get? To me, the folks who make these decisions need to get out more often. I think they insult those people by telling them, 'No. No. You're not smart enough to understand this. You should be feeling really horrible about it.' It's ridiculous.

Jeb Bush, Governor of Florida *

*St. Petersburg (Fla.) Times, August 10, 2005

V.

ms. brooks urged me to return to school
from the nervous backseat of my mustang
in 1994. but what triggered the movement
was an enid, oklahoma drunken conversation
in a honky tonk with friends from high school,
all white and pseudo-liberal. we deliberated
level playing fields & jesse jackson
while the sad child of hank williams warbled
something loud about loneliness. just as twelve
years prior, i was cultural diversity at the table
and no longer comfortable. one man, maybe
my closest oklahomey in the bar, assured me
the residuals of chattel slavery no longer existed,
while leaning against the door of a 100-year-old
family business. i enrolled in african american
studies two months later. he will not remember
this exchange any more than he will recall the night
i was informed my blackness was a liability
in his pursuit of teenage pussy. history will tell on you.

smolder

aunt 'ree has lived
through the mississippi
of sheeted heads
soiling family hands

she say
he got a white face
but he got blood
just like mine

she prays for better days
in the ashes of 1996
while a cross burns
the saints' meeting place

safe

he ate boogers and smelled like pee
the two scraggly goats looked inbred
as well   virgil's daddy the definition

of jiffy cornbread but too fucking mean
to keep weight   pitbull venom
every fourth word nasty and loud

as a monster truck   more afraid
of their house than his pops   nauseous carpet
cigarette wallpaper   a pasty white poverty

with bent hinges   virgil's mama
his father's sister   her fear gathered double
chins   i heard the beatings   three houses

down and across 10th   virgil curdling blood
out back   goats gnaw a baby doll leg
no school break   an ignorance bullies

found as duty   little sister screams like fists

government springs
after a photo of my sister Charolette circa 1960

what is she looking for, clay
mare solemn in stagnation,
going nowhere forward.
sunday-dressed all patent
leather and lace stiff. behind her
a calling, an earth upturned
by lineage, garden fed musty
promise, cheap whiskey. and what lies
ahead: swings, a merry-go-round (where's the
horse for a kid that's black?), the chatter
of relentless monkeys. an amusement
park, wpa constructed, where teenage
girls wrap poles every may. did she see
herself integrating the orchestra, afro big
as a violin. fierce serious on her face,
learned behavior. a hard look
at missteps not to follow. later, on stage
with panthers on the lam, she'd raise
a fist, unearth a poet's hand.

cleaning graves in calvert
for Papa Johnny Hodge, my Great-Great Grandfather

under a crying elder willow
we meet the 107 degree shade
bearing thirsty earth
from which i sprang

a safehouse next door to
a tinderbox church
sanctuary from hot

lone star nights.
though your face is hidden
i feel you in the folds

calling beyond the tired summer
crops to bring us here

we were last to know
ritual precedes emancipation

harvest

yellow-gold overgrowth

wheat like children raising
arms high to be picked. everywhere
is shaft scraping cloud, every
where is nowhere, what's behind
looks like what's ahead.

a boy no more than twelve
commanding earth, tiny monarch
in green glass, a southwestern
pope-mobile sweating progress.

the smooth hand of machine.

after harvest

from mullet to buzz cut

used up breadbasket for a world
that barely cares, tips cereal
box. braided rows half unkempt, tossed
by god's breathing. jagged stubble
in blistering sun, the almost

bald head endless flat. mane cropped
by fortress that blocks traffic in both
directions. vaulted cockpit a telephone
booth with hips, helix of blade a sinister grin

idle, only sky to fill time.

blur

sulking two lane highway
herefords and steer wave
sad, watery eyes, mouth
mouthfuls of bad manners.

this mid-sized sportscar
momentary thrill, quick
escape from mulch, ominous
future. a crimson valley

just beyond the fading idea
of intersection, karen silkwood's pale
imprint—lifeless silos, limping
tallgrass. a town named crescent

struggling to recover after death
her murder wrought three decades
gone. speed zone—55, 45, then 35
now 25, pentecostal church, bowing

a-frames, tasty treet, jail, post
office, then 35, 45, 55, 70—a memory
withering on the roadside.

anadarko blue

sunday hung out by the corner
with nowhere to go

without concern
for changing events

or turning stomachs
brotha's huddling in a parking lot

passing a spliff
and eating church's chicken

you weren't home

blind

arnita was slow   girth and mind   open window the call   train whistle

not my crowd   knew who they were   where she lived   dirt road

wretch   poor house lean   which rich white boy   bait exchange

she gifted   snack packs   twinkies   in jeeps polo   cross border

eastside creep   your alone   head with no face   rode past once

drunk   late bloom   no stop   curtain trembles   night wind

crescent, ok

the true sense of humankind's will
is measured by grey days in early december
when stagnant pools evolve from slouching drizzle

skies of sunday melancholia
highway seventy-four south
quilted patches of green and red
weave the horizon in rusting ingenuity

standing still a tempo

playing hooky
for jimbo

sitting here with you watching
middle america gnaw on itself

newlyweds roll their newborn
past a silver speedboat

its sleek design, promise of adventure
a cadence that sways listless pines

gully

a shallow pond the remains dregs
under an oak canopy with poor posture
branches spindly varicose fingers
nudging dribble of soggy earth

breasted wrens shuffle nod at soil
rusty brown-green to the east a tangle
natty dreds of broken limbs make
guessing game of sunlight

here now there shadowplay
a somber red dirt lyric
patchy knot grass and twigs
subterfuge for rattler hole

in crusty terra on the bank
or what would be if water
stood deeper than this thought
a slight breeze lists the elders

pilgrimage

body africa is almost sick almost
healthy thin about the waist bone
weak to bone belligerent joints
frantic memory perpetual fever

and again the desert's toothless mouth
as weathered palm rouge to solemn
bronze *nothing is moving* she whispers
only sand that bears your name

the mediterranean makes its point: i am not
where you are algeria's glassy forehead
to furrowed brow the sahara's hot breath
incessant stutter dusky cough of cloud

older here sun wrinkles
toward ocean weary of moon
i long to kiss the endless
horizon the sediment of our sons

ankle high in questions

II.   muddy bloodline

circumstance

i don't even drink
beer, but there it is
a sagging bag. contents:

catfish after midnight
lounging tofutti

late attention paid
after sons are asleep
wife unloads day

the weight of love.

i eat imitation moonlight
disguised as soy. think
healthy. dream of push-ups.

lonely offices

it is two a.m. mewling
son cribbed next to mama
three older brothers

a short dark hall away
in sleeping bag cocoons
yet to bed papa descends

the boiler begs water
twenty below   a duppy
has crept through kitchen

knocked student essays
from desk baiting him
to junky basement

groaning wooden stairs
light switch memories
mold in boxes hang

from pipes spill about
the floor almost clutter
hope almost promise

by dawn our bodies will
disremember shiver
hardwood snug underfoot

wedlock
for kelly

she bounds down stairs at 7:30
our toddler navigating one flight to the sitter
two winterized sons waiting.
twenty-five unkind minutes of highway
between now and school bell.

after making breakfast, packing lunchboxes
stuffing backpacks and zipping bubble coats
i stand half-naked in the bathroom entryway
brushing teeth while pondering an 8:00 appointment
with a brother named spq (pronounced *speak*) about dreads.

she bristles up stairs at 7:33
asks, from same doorway, if i'd deliver
cough medicine to sitter upon departure,
questioning me less than three feet from the bottle,
his lung rattle wafting through the open front door.

i consent. she runs down stairs at 7:34,
passes the sitter's, the phlegmy air,
then, boys in her wake, plunges headfirst
into swearword cold chicago morning.

she is on time. i am late.

running in place

my six month old son
is snoring. at 2:30 a.m.
this breath brings memory:
the must of hangover
while television watches daddy
sleep off another two-day retreat.
the cowboys-eagles game unfolds.

upright by the easy chair,
his boots taunt me.
the muddy cowhide murmur
tales of red clay & big sky
only to find themselves here.
their point is mockery;
such confidence of direction,

purpose. here, alone
with these menacing boots,
their fresh dirt and daddy's
snoring. at 2:37 a.m.
my son changes position.

crutch

when i was younger
most of the men i knew

couldn't stand up straight
couldn't bend their knees

they struggled to walk
gravity against them

in my teens
it was cool to pimp

one leg with purpose
the other wandered lazily

now young men move
swiftly one leg with purpose

the other stiff and loaded
i am older   my limbs remember

uncle lawrence's canes
rest at the bottom of the stairs

wither
for Pops, for Mary

1.

tuesday, storms uprooted her
fifty year old american elm.

eyes glassy ponds,
nervous throat. she knows

i 'm sad, but doesn't think
i care. trees are not worthy.

2.

two arteries drip on my father's brain
without tiring. surgeons suggest detours,

stomach reservoir. talk of shunts,
flow, distilling time.

3.

men bring machines,
resolve. leave a hole.

4.

her words on my shoulder
slouch like splintered limbs.

my father's room

where we begin end
i look at you   see our face:

stark wallpaper a mental prison
rorschach blots taint cells of wilting
synapse   sputtering wattage

you call me with your eyes
alone we unravel what is left

braille

high on pcp, in-law beat sis until eyes
knotted. threw wall at my niece

then called daddy to boast handiwork
long distance murder threats

fifteen miles between them.
my sister's face raising

the mississippi in daddy's veins.
big sis and niece feel their way

through swollen night
drive into an elm tree, crawl

to the old pastor's door.
he was two counties gone

when paramedics offered reasons
to live, gave me reason to kill.

daddy's river a muddy bloodline.

crack

if poets are to be consumed by it
you are hayden with empty pen

brooks, in ache for streets
etch gray verse on blank skin

brown, want of strong men
rib cage guards stale smoke

your hunger for death chokes us

crack house

greeter

she hustles us in
eyes tired

shadows stutter
behind nervous trees

outer room

screen door grime
a porous portal

paneling drips
frantic carpet

living room

up early ricki lake
an endless loop

tv's wide blue mouth
the only thing moving

pantry

she fast food she
buy one get one free

kitchen

parched bones
silently akimbo

peel of burn
gray of skin

he sizzles
cooks

orphan

my dreams sleep in beds they have outgrown
nightmares leave room enough for any soul
i am the size of my own hollow promise
flush with life despite the darkening night

the preacher prays for me her vacant psalms
church fan perfect with a cutting smile
message unholy, steam rises from lips
why can't we speak the grace we all avoid?

might we choose a path the prophet walked?
mama knew the way to seek pure light
now i find me in her waning breath
wandering toward them with baby steps

i am anew, born in the pain of death
god forbid i lose all i have learned

haunted
for Agha Shahid Ali

on a train reading shahid's poems
about his mother's death thinking of mine

at a festival in virginia he crowned me
ali #2, then flirted relentlessly

in indiana, where radio is a lonely
place, i linger on our mothers, shahid

and how home is not when mama's gone
spit of smoke and powerlines ornate

birdless dusk, the burnt tar odor of gasping
midwestern ideas. even football field lights

dim this friday. brother this *is* my birthplace
born like this with dirt in my hair

if we were lovers we'd visit oklahoma
my father loathing your manliness

mama admiring your soap opera vocabulary
my parents are gone, shahid, as are you and yours

Thus I swear, here and now, not to forgive the universe
that would let me get used to a universe

without you…

mama sense: an elegy

scent

mama was loud, a live broadcast
the weather always spring

on her neck and bosom
she worked 3-11, so weekends

i watched her wrestle skirts over slips
long & white, check hose for runs

blouse and smock latched, the sugary
mist, flower water in angled ray and shadow

tiny shards rode parched afternoon
between tired beige curtains

touch

labor to find the words
an uneasy freedom jitters

of a woman whose core was salt
divine as laughter i spoke them

first new language to our dialect
twenty-four years lived in geography

and telephone wire changed little she
became awkward as adolescence

i was teenage smooth from town she
big-boned farm girl with smile vast

as texas *i love you mama* later
she let me hold her hand

sight

morning night finds me
in chatter with a flirting star

kiss skin of dream linger
as calm trees utter your name

it has not rained in days
bruised sun whispers storm to quiet

sound

my second son came quietly sixty
seconds before blue flushed red

has not stopped talking since his
tongue a net of lost time mama's

song only lessened the volume her tones
his colicky pillow rooted hum the balm

for a two-week bad day melody nothing
you know yet every cell swears it gospel

taste

after your mama dies
there is no guarantee
anyone will pray for you

III.   where we live

.

eulogy two

we met on the first day of basketball practice at the armory. it was 1973. third grade. had round, short bodies; were forwards, you right of the paint, me left. we sucked. but made one another laugh and loved the game. we continued to be third string in almost every sport except the ability to laugh in the midst of madness. except life. twenty-seven years. you brought me bay city rollers and abba. i brought you earth, wind & fire. black boy and white boy in smalltown usa with an uneasy past. in 1975, my school closed due to desegregation. we became classmates. clowns competing for the highest gpa. i received the award for academic achievement, you the model student-citizen. so inseparable some thought us gay in junior high. was your high school cyrano. russ, you are my first love. you taught me courtesy and humility. i gave you freedom to be who you are, who you were.

give and go

this united center
was outside, my backdoor
backyard arena packed
sundays sweaty. swearing

jabbar stood closer to god
than moses, i witnessed
gravity turned sideways
by high school brotha's

in knee high tube socks.
i collected their moves
like germs on a six year old:
lacey's shake and bake,

clifford's turnaround in-yo-face,
dewayne's deadly twenty-footer, and
crazy cousin larry's baby
sky hook, which could never be

released without calling his name:
uh-oh, it's kareem abdul-jabbar
with the unstoppable hook shot!,
larry would scream, one thirteen inch

foot over my head. the big boys
let me hang because of dede,
my sister, who they all liked.
besides, it was my yard and

my goal. even though larry
nailed the hoop too high
on the backboard, i learned
to play big with my squat body,

and grew to appreciate the metaphor.

police

you had a dog named snowball that smelled funny and suffered
from tooth decay. she was your eldest sister's dog. snowball was
very old. never liked that dog. not because she was ancient or
smelled like sewer. because she came out when you had to go in.
long white dog of the law.

halloween

when it was time for your dad's funeral
my folks brought me new shoes
flared jeans empty excuses

perched on the top stair
i screamed salty words

you didn't really forget
you just don't want me to go

white sneakers like rain

later i spoke with your mom
apologized for not being there
asked what could i do

she said be there so i was
at eight to sit with you
while jamie lee curtis

took our minds off death

eulogy three

should have never introduced you. blonde thin and fire. your type. my homegirl knew her. didn't see you again for a year and a half. had four classes together. fire resented our bond. denied access. saw you when banging head to concrete. worried about conception. when fire got too hot. the second time was freshman year of college, end of first semester. you were moving out to live with mike. snoring reminded you of deceased father, gone four years. i also refused to follow as did your new family, who were not new. girlfriend and two sidekicks, all holdovers from high school. hooked you up with girlfriend, whom i liked first. was over that. never close to tweedle-dee and dum. we were brothers. equals. you changed. came back upon meeting my new crew: punk rockers, artists, alternative thinkers. didn't leave again until falling in love with my ex (it occurs to me now we were an incestuous lot). moved out to be with her without me. never said why. found out in newspaper newsroom. tweedle-dee with you two, too. you abandoned me three times in twenty seven years. you always came back. come back now.

after the concert

you made it to school second period
mr. milacek's psychology class

how ya doin, rusty?
enjoy the show?

red eyes mumbled low
hand to head as you throbbed
down the aisle

we laughed at the brain
cells spinning at your feet

pre-game rituals

after weighing the sugar content
of greensprings and boones farm
the press box didn't seem so high
my ascent noted by well-wishers

mr. clausing skulks the doorway
explains how sound travels   pauses
travels back this gridiron valley
prayer in hand reeks of stale grapes

i open my mouth   its volume
wide as friday night   aunt bonnell's words
in my voice careen off the far side
return in white light

woozy i sway into the text
petition for harmless battle
good sportsmanship and grace
dodging myself like a boxer

rowdy friends gather in bleachers
share my joy   you are there so is she
never thought she'd come between
lately such an evil spirit

on the day of the harmonic convergence

> a 1972 audi fox (known as
> the sun car because my homeys
> cut out most of the roof and its hue)
> which had sat idle for eight months
> started without a second thought

it was elvis' birthday

> and though we knew this we didn't realize
> until we drove to the store (in russ' ride--
> the sun car set half a block earlier)
> to learn royalty was in the park

all the planets aligned

> it was not our fault they became angry at us
> laughing at the poor excuse for a dead king
> jiggling pasty flesh in august heat

it was not coincidence

> we went back to the purple basement
> built a shrine to capture music
> between us felt earth push and spin

last time alive
christmas 1999, enid, ok

we snuck away to buy beer
smokes get high then

returned to opposite rooms:
you to a wife that sweatered

your winter; me to referee
small boys and tonka trucks

you'd only met my sons
hours earlier our years

of dreaming in tiny hands
never knew your heart

in the photo we wear the same smile

xmas past
union square park, december 2002

i return to the place
i came when you left me
here. it's christmas.
i sit and wander
dreaming to find you.

we'd meet at your house
after presents and family.
i'd show you my bike
(a new one three years
in a row coz carlos stole
them) and you'd share
farrah in bikini and teeth.

today, i brought scars.

eulogy one

what was on your heart when the moss gave way. when you slid
off that table rock. before the gorge snapped your back. before
your body found the pool of the first waterfall, eight-five feet
below. was it julie, who watched the soles of your boots vanish
then held her breath thirty days until nature chose to share. or
mama hutchison, chain smoking in the house on beverly she
bought after your father passed. i pray it was grace. i yelped at
the new york moon for you, brother. held vigil in union square
whispering to smoke. nailed your image on trees. you came,
finally, all calm and cold, with permission to write our handhold.
corpus cristi or winston-salem. chicago or brooklyn. no matter.
this will always be where we live.

why i hate boston

because the moment i stepped out
the car a human failed to recognize my being

because abdul-jabbar's lakers
were my team in the early seventies

because dr. j's sixers were
my team in the late seventies

because of john havlicek and larry bird

(i should give the celtics some love
   due to bill russell, but reserve that love for him)

because we could see the building
but spiraled dumbfounded for an hour

because of buses

because of middle aged graying poets
who've earned a southside beatdown

because it is a different cold

because it is a playground for dominant culture

because of tom brady and bill belichick

(for the record, i'm ok with the red sox
   as long as they keep manny & big papi)

because every high school morning
russ cranked *don't look back*

because i'd move to the damned fenway
for the chance to hear him sing with brad delp

nature
wichita mountains, medicine park, ok

we hiked over an hour
cockleburs question our ankles

sweat bleeds dry sun
tears our somber ascent

summit elbows cloud
gorge a wide red grin

river drools miles below

tod unwrapped the plastic
around you   kissed god

gave half of you back
then handed me the urn

i guided you to sky
you refused to leave

grit of you in my mouth

IV. parting water

eighth grade

I.

teens in kalamazoo tell me
words that spark indifference:
nigger (note spelling), bitch,
hoe (note spelling), then confirm
emcee's spat those lyrics at them
that week, that morning

II.

the n-word slouches with phonics:
er is insult, *a* is family. only
marshall mathers & other
bi-racial people can drop
nig*a* and not get beat down

III.

a nervous young man, who loves
rap, shows me his essay in confidence,
declines to read it to the class
they won't understand, they'll tease me
feels white boy is as bad as nigger
in the mouth of the beholder

IV.

it means *female dog* and since she is not
she can endure the gathering
of hooded nike superheroes
who meet on fabulous corners
to consider every woman but her

she, herself also super, possesses
the ability to separate beat from lyric,
is certain fifty took all nine bullets,
of michael jackson's guilt, tupac's breath

public   **school**

runny nose   hormones
anxious reason   tense laughter
jigga what   man size
sagging light   vacant lot
long fuse   short trigger

african america

chunky girlchild swings
hips in street, a moving
traffic, body of drum
and horn. no crosswalk
to direct flow but contrapuntal
void a conversation
at gunpoint. transient script
a purposeful noise, food
for bootyshake. most don't
know the language. life
out loud.

dead dead
heat on the southside

I.

last night, police cordoned the four square
blocks surrounding my house in pursuit of a thug
who unloaded on the shell of a gangsta
in the funeral parlor filled with formaldehyde
and lead. black folks scattered, staining
complicated streets. i settle in for summer:
the maze to the front door, running teens
from my stoop smelling of weed and tragedy
reminding my sons they are not sources
of admiration, praying that might change. not yet
june heat rises like the murder rate, gleam
and pop already midnight's bitter tune

II.

fifteen years ago, tyehimba jess
told me about a funeral home
with a drive through window.

you pull up, push a call button
through bulletproof glass a friendly
somber attendant takes your request.

moments later, casket open
your order appears for review.

at the time i thought it inhumane.
now i think about the abstraction
of friendship while counting bullets.

III.

is there an extra dead?
what is the term for dying again
when already? killing chi?

and what of the corpses that walk
my block in the anonymity
of black skin and white tees
filled with fluid?

body shop

i've heard tell of a hustle
in brooklyn where clever folks
throw themselves in front of cars
lurching down eastern parkway

not the beat-up green mini-vans
or duct tape toyotas of poets, not
impalas bleeding chrome
spinning disposable testosterone

but mid to high end machines
of certain insurance booty, drivers
in the 30 to 50 year range, same
demographic as oprah's audience

i suppose there is a right and wrong
approach to this science, the angles
of minimal damage to consider, side
to bumper, back to door, head up

unless her poodle is well groomed.
few have retired, i would speculate
but work less now that checks
lack bounce and the mailman walks briskly

it must be the eyes, wide and clean
that distinguish these impact alvin aileys
from ordinary jaywalkers

at utica i marvel at the desperate genius
the split-second calculus, the risks and gains
of such occupation, before descent
into the dark anonymity of the 4 train

reverse commute
for the burnout table

clock clanks inches
southward i wander

dance on tracks
like huck's jim

a woman nears
the tree-lined path

i clutch my bag
she sees bigger

in ill-fitting darkness
i see temporary harbor

bleached in halogen
at 8:17 the 8:13

train as suburbia
groves glens brooks

dusk in our hair
busy with nothing

city rushes to greet
wearing pungent night

association

at a funeral back home i saw an old
college roommate, suburban dude, psych
phd. we called him mister posh perrier
in our waning undergraduate days
as he moved away from communal
artist poverty back to his origins before
the rest of us had decent credit scores.

we have lived within the same city limits
for over a decade. dopplegangers in private
practice dotting the near counties. tried
to uncover him years ago. here he is,
in a mourner's backyard, talking
millions, selling houses and condos
blocks from my oldest sons' school. we

are locked door, nightly news, ebonic sound
bite. drunk, i take his card, divulge my plan
to drop him on west madison after dark.
tour a chicago with no banks and scarce
fresh produce. rattle his republic, survey
millions who might benefit from pedigree.

sport

I.

this photographer's weekly work is peddling
virility: soft porn by day, pro ball nights
and weekends. eyes itchy from the substance
of dreams he slumps into a glass of vodka

there are no flaws in fantasy

then slurs colleagues follow barack's every
move. i have seen them, south lake
shore drive a parting water at dusk—
six motorcycles, three homeland security
impalas, white and blue, two khaki mini-
buses, four limos, smoke. barrels aimed
cellulose snap and burn, a neck in a rag top.

II.

populism is pejorative: one man's
community is another's advancing
army. niggas of mass destruction.
so what do we do with this?

III.

said one of his buddies shot two
frames all day. *why waste film?*

IV.

i am sooner red, a native of the most
right state in the confederation. shamefully
almost as geeked my school will vie for the title
as i am barack gracefully corrected pundits. the bcs
is like benefiting from a bad call. this time sooners
found good fortune and a heisman. in a moment
of deep tragedy i revisited my freshman yearbook:
switzer's eroding might, wayman tisdale and marcus
dupree. old new faces, my two best friends alive. on
fraternity row, halloween 1982, white boy as kkk, as
west african, as uncle ben. 1976 the last year sun
didn't set on blacks in norman. think of all the games
won by then.

V.

spent the entire campaign deflecting this mad
prophecy more probable than fiction. the country
suffers from narcolepsy and gout, with side
effects from the medicine. they are growing
in number. so are we. they all look alike.
we do not. they comfort in closed hands.
ours are open and many. get that picture.

this is not a political poem (it's about vermin)

there *is* a rodent problem in dc--
even adams-morgan   living creatures avoid
anything with dupont on the label so that
quadrant is free and clear   this is not rhetoric
this is simply ugly like the word *hemorrhoid*

texas justice is infallible   cheap speech for the hunted
blacks were happier during slavery   more compelling
script a smooth jazz an elevator music
(my old sax playing homey said *'the next time*
you hear smooth jazz ask yourself what's been
smoothed over.')

i feel for both mouse and rat   but how to know
which to befriend? ben was easy to love
(he had a soundtrack) but willard was a muthafuka

city of bones
after August Wilson

in this town where no one wants to die
the crime rate is low everyone
clothed fed to belly full medicine
bountiful young people all
challenged to limit of potential a system
to support aptitude fresh air
& produce in our town women & girls
revered cherished protected men
gracious sensitive fitness prayer in multiple
tongue prison is those who do not
believe streets safe & clean a brotha
can get a cab free shuttle for the too high
in our town where no one wants
to die news always polite *the world played*
nice today…details at 10 no sickness starvation
lonely avoid walking on neighbors
lawn taxes paid on time haiti japan
spared all of us superheroes all of us
ordinary this town
not cairo madison tehran
no fly zone no gangs we assemble peace
gather in tiny or public space say excuse me
we are post race   no history beyond right
now maybe yesterday we can't remember

september eleven, two-thousand and two

I.

the man sitting across
the aisle: sandy blonde,
smirnoff smile, polo glasses,
fiftyish, tells me he wears it
every time he hops a plane.

the star spangled grips
his love handles.

i wonder if this cotton
harbors his children. if
this t-shirt is his coffin.

he smiles. says
his cape is overhead

II.

my ears popping, racist
crossfire, a hot subway
car, the shakes of old
west indian women,
wall street's eclipse.

III.

a roll of beige shag,
full-bellied moans,
violent contractions,

her attempts at breath,
prayer in damp eyes,
countless wounded
spirits, one white phone.

IV.

the ash of us.

millions of half-dead
grey moving through winter-
still toward the sun's
new brooklyn home.

the elder's heart attack face,
the bridge too much to bear,
humanity too much to cross,
medics buzz both shores.

V.

my brother-in-law is a fed.

worked at the murrah
building, but was across
the street. moved
to the pentagon. sky
bled on his shoes.

we don't talk much.

VI.

wednesday, i will burn
my clothes (the off-white
fly collar and olive khakis),
throw away the italian leathers
i love but can't make clean.

cutting locs

I.

unkink gentle spirits
let loose these bones

my lawn of hair
scissor weed and thistle

root thorn and rubroot
my feet of hands

earthcrumbs trail stale
air trace clouds

II.

twelve years lie awake
in a wooden bowl

alive as morningsong
they reach to greet me

i rub ache and wail

III.

too many duppys
sanctuary my hair

some were invited
some fell from sky

IV.

follicles womb supple
nest floor reborn

we are flight

About the Poet

Quraysh Ali Lansana is author of six poetry books, three textbooks, a children's book, editor of eight anthologies, and coauthor of a book of pedagogy. He is Associate Professor of English/Creative Writing at Chicago State University, where he served as Director of the Gwendolyn Brooks Center for Black Literature and Creative Writing from 2002-2011. *Our Difficult Sunlight: A Guide to Poetry, Literacy & Social Justice in Classroom & Community* (with Georgia A. Popoff) was published in March 2011 by Teachers & Writers Collaborative and was a 2012 NAACP Image Award nominee.